Holidays and Celebrations
Easter

by Brenda Haugen
illustrated by Sheree Boyd

Thanks to our advisers for their expertise, research, and advice:

Alexa Sandmann, Ed.D., Professor of Literacy
The University of Toledo, Toledo, Ohio
Member, National Council for the Social Studies

Susan Kesselring, M.A., Literacy Educator
Rosemount-Apple Valley-Eagan (Minnesota) School District

PICTURE WINDOW BOOKS
MINNEAPOLIS, MINNESOTA

For Ellen, my bunny-sitter

Managing Editor: Bob Temple
Creative Director: Terri Foley
Editor: Sara E. Hoffmann
Editorial Adviser: Andrea Cascardi
Copy Editor: Laurie Kahn
Designer: Melissa Voda
Page production: The Design Lab
The illustrations in this book were rendered digitally.

Picture Window Books
5115 Excelsior Boulevard
Suite 232
Minneapolis, MN 55416
1-877-845-8392
www.picturewindowbooks.com

Printed in the United States of America.

Library of Congress Cataloging-in-Publication Data
Haugen, Brenda.
Easter / by Brenda Haugen ; illustrated by Sheree Boyd.
p. cm. — (Holidays and celebrations)
Summary: Briefly discusses the history and customs connected
to the celebration of Easter.
Includes bibliographical references.
ISBN 1-4048-0194-4
1. Easter—Juvenile literature. [1. Easter. 2. Holidays.] I. Boyd, Sheree,
ill. II. Title. III. Holidays and celebrations (Picture Window Books)
GT4935 .H34 2004
394.2667—dc21
                                        2003006105

Plants are poking their little heads out of the ground.
Birds are chirping merrily.

3

Children are dressed in fancy new clothes.
It must be Easter!

Easter is a Christian holiday. It celebrates the life of Jesus Christ. For Christians, Easter is the holiest day of the year.

Many families celebrate Easter by going to church. Then they come home and have a big feast.

Long ago, people in England started serving ham at their Easter feasts. Some English people moved to the United States and brought this custom with them. Now, many people in the United States serve ham on Easter.

Lamb, chicken, and turkey are other popular Easter meals. Many homes are filled with delicious smells on this day!

A popular Easter treat is hot cross buns. Hot cross buns are yummy and sweet.

On the top of hot cross buns are white crosses made of icing. This is how they got their name.

In many countries, people eat pretty Easter cakes. People in Greece and Russia share Easter cakes with their friends and families.

11

Easter also is a celebration of spring.

Spring is a time of new life.
Many baby animals
are born in the spring.

Eggs are symbols of new life. In the spring, many animals hatch from eggs.

Easter eggs are symbols of life, too. Children color them purple, pink, orange, and green. People first colored eggs at spring festivals. The colored eggs reminded people of spring's sunlight.

Children all around the world love Easter egg hunts. The hunts are much like the games people played centuries ago in the springtime.

Easter egg-rolling contests are an ancient custom. People rolled eggs across the ground and tried not to break them.

Some people still celebrate Easter with Easter egg rolls. In the United States, the White House holds an Easter egg roll on the lawn. Children use ladles, or spoons, to roll eggs across the grass.

Some children wake on Easter morning to find special surprises. The Easter Bunny has left them baskets full of goodies!

Children find chocolate bunnies, jelly beans, and even toys in their baskets.

Long ago, German children made nests in their gardens for the Easter Bunny. Years later, many Germans moved to the United States and Canada. They brought this tradition with them. This is how the custom of Easter baskets started.

Easter is a celebration of life.
It is a time to be thankful.

Go on an Easter egg hunt.
Enjoy a chocolate bunny.
It's Easter!

You Can Make an Easter Bunny Puppet

What you need:

several sheets of construction
   paper (different colors)

scissors

small brown paper bag

glue

white cotton ball

What you do:

1. Make sure you have an adult to help you.
2. Using several sheets of construction paper, cut out ears, eyes, whiskers, a mouth, and a nose for your bunny.
3. Open the paper bag and turn it upside down. This will be your bunny's body.
4. Decorate the bag by gluing the construction-paper cutouts onto it.
5. Glue the cotton ball on the back of the bag. This is your bunny's tail.
6. Put your hand inside the bag. You have an Easter Bunny puppet!

Fun Facts

- Americans spend about $1 billion on Easter candy each year.

- In China, parents of new babies traditionally gave red eggs to relatives and friends. The eggs symbolize new life, and red is the color of fortune and happiness.

- Easter falls on a different Sunday each year. In the Protestant and Catholic churches, Easter is between March 22 and April 25. People of the Greek Orthodox faith celebrate Easter according to a different calendar.

- Lilies are traditional Easter flowers. Millions of Easter lilies are grown each year. Gardeners plant the flowers in time for them to bloom around Easter.

- English people once believed it was bad luck to wear old clothes on Easter Sunday. Many people still buy new outfits each year to wear for Easter.

Words to Know

Christian—a person who follows the teachings of Jesus Christ

feast—a big meal

festival—a special celebration. Long ago, people held festivals to celebrate spring.

symbol—something that stands for something else

tradition—a belief or custom handed down to children from their parents

To Learn More

At the Library

Gibbons, Gail. **Easter**. New York: Holiday House, 1989.

Kalman, Bobbie. **We Celebrate Easter**. New York: Crabtree Pub. Co., 1985.

Schuh, Mari C. **Easter**. Mankato, Minn.: Pebble Books, 2003.

Van Straalen, Alice. **The Book of Holidays Around the World**. New York: Dutton, 1986.

Wing, Natasha. **The Night Before Easter**. New York: Grosset & Dunlap, 1999.

Fact Hound

Fact Hound offers a safe, fun way to find Web sites related to this book. All of the sites on Fact Hound have been researched by our staff.
http://www.facthound.com

1. Visit the Fact Hound home page.
2. Enter a search word related to this book, or type in this special code: 1404801944.
3. Click on the FETCH IT button.

Your trusty Fact Hound will fetch the best sites for you!

Index